AMAZING UNIVERSE

THE SECRETS OF THE UNIVERSE

SPIRIT WORLD

"CLOUD ATLAS"

Volume 2

A BOOK OF BEAUTIFUL PHOTOS OF THE

SPIRITS & MYSTERIOUS MYSTERIES

OF THE PLANET

NEVER BEFORE SEEN PHOTOS

Table of Contents

Acknowledgments

I would like to thank the creator of the universe (the one source).

For the wisdom and knowledge to give back to the world.

My parent for the positive words and the lesson as a child in the Christian religion.

To my editor and publisher, Mathew, you rock! Thanks for putting up with my indisiveness. You're awesome!

And last but far from least, myself. For believing enough in me to write a book about this marvelous, mysterious planet Earth, we live on.

I love you all!

Dedication

In the words of the late Louis Armstrong.

What a wonderful world

I see trees of green. Red roses, too. I see them blossom from me to you. And I think to

myself. What a wonderful world.

I see skies of blue and clouds of white. The bright, blessed day. The dark, sacred night.

And I think to myself what a wonderful world.

The colors of the rainbow, so pretty in the sky, are also on the faces of the people going by.

I see a friend shaking hands, saying how do you do? They are all saying I love you!

I heard babies cry; I watched them grow. They'll learn much more than I'll ever know.

And I think to myself.

"what a wonderful world.

Louie Armstrong,
1901- July 6. 1971

About the Author

I grew up in a small town in Perris, California; in 1964, the population was 2,950, and most of the people were farmers. I grew up on a farm. The town has truly flourished now, with 81,399 population.

My parents were dedicated Christian folks who had three family churches. My cousin Rev Artis, uncle, Uncle Jesse, and aunty, Aunt Bird. (Arkansas).

All pastors with a nice congregation.

I was destined for spirituality. We attended my uncle's church, a Pentecostal Pastor. Morning, noon and nighttime, I can remember falling asleep on my mom's lap late at night. They would just lay you on the floor and put a blanket over you. I was about 3 or 4 years of age. I was so in love with God. Growing up, I was an introvert. Did not really speak or talk that much. Unless you were asking me a question, I was very watchful and shy even through secondary school. Not knowing how to express my thoughts was an issue.

This led to some people taking advantage of my innocence.

My dreams were always spiritual as a child. Always dream of dead people that have passed. Some I knew well, some I did not. They would ask me to convey a message to a loved one who would be suffering from the death or loss of a family member. My dreams are so often they begin to scare me. I did not inner stand the spirit realm as I do now.

At 19, I got saved (devoted my life to God), as they would say, at my cousin's church.

Thank you,

I was on the road to becoming a Missionary, a soul winner for Christ. I was also a Sunday school teacher and a Vocational Bible School Teacher, and through all the teaching and learning, a process started inside of me.

At 27 years old, I married a Muslim. I raised my three children in Islam vegetarian; we were vegetarian.

We prayed five times a day. No Christmas, No pork, No Jesus. After having been together for almost ten or 11 years, we divorced. He was involved.

After my divorce, I chose to work on myself. I began to focus more on my spiritual quest, reading and searching everything from history, religion, numerology, Anunnaki, Greek mythology, African heritage, and anything related to knowledge. I became a sponge. The thirst was on. I had discovered my purpose in life. I love the mystery of the earth, the hidden spiritual parts, the unseen universe. I was finally free. From all the past hurts, from society's opinions, and most of all, from the devil. Through it all, I have learned that religion keeps you in fear. I am now a free thinker.

Admiration

I have always been a fan of the sky. The clouds, how they all seem to be just watching over humanity. I truly do understand the bible. When it says Jesus will return on a cloud.

They can be so captivating. Soft, angelic, and beautiful.

They are filled with amazement. The world we live in is full of secret and unknown magisteries that sometimes aid us in our spiritual quest or journey as well as ascension.

Several of the forces of the universe are observing life as we live it. The watcher.

The gods in the sky. Have you ever wondered how the creator knows all? The all-knowing. How everything is recorded, even your thoughts, the words you speak in private, daydreams. You know the saying we are never alone; it is a true statement.

There are things unseen all around us. I am convinced that if we were to observe the unseen force that governs our planet, with our own understanding. We would be frightened or repelled by the things beyond our imaginations.

We have things like fairies. Do you believe in the fairy's kingdom? Goblins and magical squirrels, gnomes,

I am sitting here laughing to myself because I always wanted to believe in fairy tales.

I have found out that there is always some truth to every legend.

Fairies, gnomes and creatures. They are all-embracing here, on earth (mother gaia). There is only one consciousness, and they are very afraid of humans.

Human always seems to destroy or dissect things that are beyond their inner-standings.

They seek to rule control for riches, popularity gain, or stardom and fame.

In this book, we will touch on the spiritual side of the planet. The gods in the sky, watching over humankind.

This earth we live on is so beautiful and amazing.

I don't know much, but I am learning and receiving knowledge from sources every day.

Ase'

"what if life is the dream? And when we die, we wake up!"

Pictures of Nature's Spirits

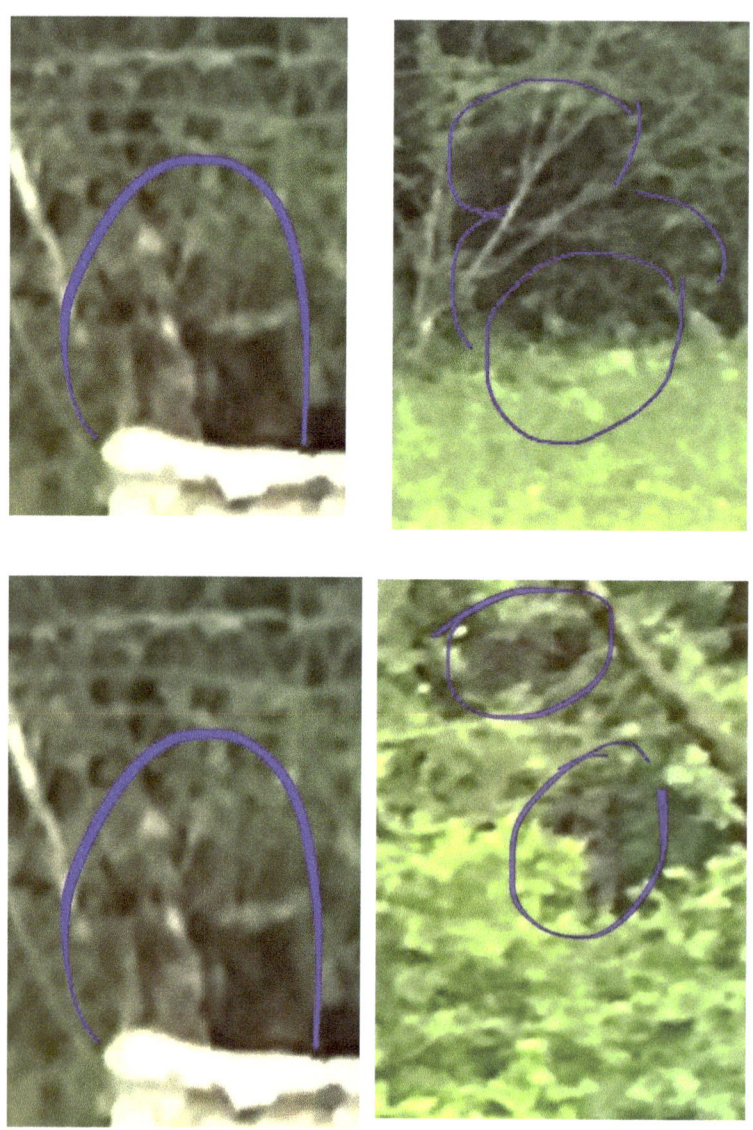

I love this beautiful planet, and I have the urgency need to tell the world it loves us as well. We are all one, with source (creator) consciousness. We are all part of the big plan of life. It's a remarkable, beautiful system. Everything we could possibly need is at our fingertips; the source has been set in place for our survival. There are enough resources on this planet to satisfy every man's needs, unfortunately, but not his greed.

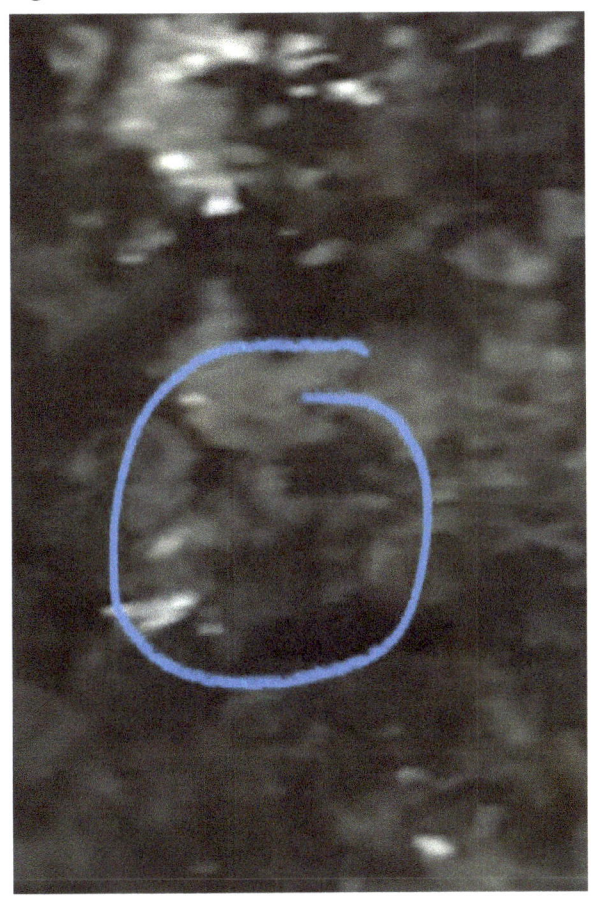

THE SOUL

"The soul is the same in all living creatures, although the body of each is different. "

Hippocrates

The soul while in a human body. Life will definitely have an effect on soul life and when you die. The soul moves to a new body this is called "transmigration."

The soul's next life (incarnation) will also be determined by its karma.

There is no difference in the soul of man than the soul of a bear or eagle. Why would there be? Every living creature is brought to creation in the same manner as humans, in a womb, sac, or egg through birth. It is the souls that quicken the body and give the life.

We are all created by the creator(god). Even though the body is different, there is only one consciousness on this planet, and that is god consciousness.

Open our hearts to inner standing, and the awakening of the veil will begin to unfold.

The earth we live on is governed by certain rules. Set forth for our rewards on earth.

Once you begin to ascend to this inner stand that all is within you, you will be amazed by the beautiful things you begin to experience. You must release all fear.

Fear is what holds us back from our gifts and blessings. False evidence appears real.

We must always be resonating in love. Love is the highest vibration. The temple of god is in your mind. Your existence always.

Why do you think they call it the temple on the side of your brain(head)? Place your mind with consciousness. You are a god source (god) that resides in the body, not on the outside.

When you give up on hope and feel that exhaustion in your body, you just cannot take it any longer, this is when the good things start to happen.

We are master creators. Created by: a master creator. A master design assigned here on earth to become a master creator.

What does that mean? It means following your heart's desire. Every man is given to him a design within. Find your (design)passions in life, the things you enjoy doing that come naturally. You have to give back some of you to the creation (the universe) so that the creator can give you back in abundance. Put the *law of inspired* action to work in your life. I guarantee you will be amazed. I wear the magic glasses proudly!

"Under the secret magical, mystical paradise, here on mother gaia. She resonates on a very high frequency. She is always evolving; if we want to evolve, the rewards are endless. You must follow the 12 laws of the universe."

Can you see the spirit of the Cardinal Bird, a beautiful woman with red hair, legend has it. They were beautiful woman cursed to live out their lives as birds.

Photograph by: Ruby Thomas

Picture of a Vulture Sitting On A Limb

Snap this photo of a Vulture in my backyard. Can you see the spirit of the Vulture? It almost looks like a pirate.

12 LAWS OF THE UNIVERSE

1. The Law of Divine Oneness.

The law of divine oneness states that we are all interconnected on this planet.

We are all connected to the one wholeness of humanity to nature, minerals. Plants.

And insects, animals and non-living matter as well. It connects all that is

Nothing exists outside of the divine oneness.

Everyone's choices, beliefs and, words, even desires will affect others.

Having an impact on the world and the people in your life. We are all connected.

2. Law of Vibration.

According to the law of vibration, everything vibrates. Moves, everything is energy. The universe is in constant rotation. This law also implies everything that has been manufactured: your microphone, table etc. All things carry a vibration. Energy attracts according to your vibrations. If you are vibrating on a low frequency, such as guilt, the ego, dishonesty, or backbiting. That's what you will attract: a low vibration, and vice versa. All particles in the universe are made of energy.

3. Law of Correspondence

If your life is out of control, check your thoughts; you control the destiny.

What happens around us is a direct reflection of what is happening within us.

4. The Law of Attraction.

The law of attraction is self-explanatory. You attract, that is, what you are in likeness to. If you are a loving person within. You will attract love; it also goes hand in hand with the law of vibration. Stay positive so that you may attrative positive vibes.

You attract what you are.

5. The Law of Inspired Actions.

Now, this is my favorite law because it took me some time to realize the word inspired was the key to returning abundance by the universe. First, the action lets us break that down.

This law is the action of the "law of attraction"; these two laws are closely related.

This is the action of putting one foot in front of the other, but you must also be inspired by your actions meaning. It is something that you do with ease and brings joy to you.

You enjoy doing it. This law states you must pursue your goals with inspired actions.

6. The Law of Perpetual Transmutation Of Energy

The transmutation of energy, meaning that if you engage on a low frequency, feeling sad, self-sabotaging and here comes your best friend vibrating full of joy and sunshine. It can change your vibration as well.

All individuals have withn them the power to change.

7. The Law of Cause And Effect

The law of cause-and-effect people don't understand. This is a danger zone for many. You get back what you send out in the universe. Blame yourself and not the devil for your shortcomings. For every action, there is a reaction.

8. The Law of Compensation

The law of compensation is about planting your seeds. Similar to the law of attraction.

This law can come as a karma or a blessing. Say you win the lottery, and you think that everything is about to be grand, just perfect. The next year, the IRS starts confiscation for back taxes you owe. Child support makes a demand for back payments because you never showed or nurtured your children. You have always been self-centered. Selfish kind of guy. This could be your worst nightmare according to the law of compensation; this law reminds us that we weep what we sow. You will receive exactly what you put out.

Be a giver, spread love, and always be thankful!

9. The Law of Relativity

The law of relativity is about how you see your circumstances in life. Nothing is good or bad, just relative.

Never see any circumstance as negative. You know it's not about blaming others or outside forces for the good or bad situations that may occur. You remain conscious of

Knowing that there is always a positive answer, multiple perspectives and positive reinforcements for anything that has happened in your life, you remain grateful to all.

10. The Law of Polarity

The law of polarity states that everything has an opposite.

11. Law of Rhythm

The law of rhythm focuses on movement. "this is the law of perpetual motions in the universe.' everything changes. Nature, seasons, growing old, infant to toddler, all things come in cycles and stages of development.

12. The Law of Gender

This law speaks of feminine and masculine energies. We all contain a vast amount of both energies and must find a way of achieving balance between them both energies, if we are to live an authentic life.

What is DHARMA?? The art of being you!

According to Krishna, he explains the karma is inevitable for all beings

Dharma is for the soul. The soul is to be kept as clean as possible from wicked actions and tendencies. These duties must be implemented in the soul. The correct ways of living.

It makes you practice what you preach.

The 5 pillars of dharma

1. **Knowledge**

2. **Patience**

3. **Love**

4. **Dedication**

5. **Justice**

Living in truth is the highest dharma and the source of all virtues. The eternal law.

ELEMENTALS, SPIRIT OF THE EARTH

Spirits of the mother gaia(earth). We have the elements, just like the cartoons.

Air, fire, water, earth, they aide in nature as well. The elements are here for nature purposes. They can also help in spiritual ways to mankind. There are some Buddhist priests who can control the elements.

These elemental spirits are not seen by humans because they operate on a different frequency. Fear blocks us from communicating with nature.

They truly respond to your energy. They are unseen forces that help Mother Nature balance the earth.

I can recall reading about a tornado that devasted the entire town to ruin all except one house. The house was also in the path of the tornado of some unseen forces; the house was untouched, and not even a window was blown out. The tornado had leveled everything in its path and more. The house was untouched by nature. I ask the question? Is this a coincidence? The family was amazed when they saw the result. A tornado of that magnitude would have devoured everything in its path. There are spirits and forced that govern over us all. And Mother Earth. She will not let you harm her she is alive.

Earth represents solidarity, everything that is tangible and everything that is solid.

Air represents the wind it carries, communication, wisdom, and knowledge.

Water represents the forever-flowing current. The emotion of love. And balance fire represents a destructive force. Untamed in nature. Represents creation, destruction, power, and protection.

Fire represents a destructive force. Untamed in nature. Also represents the creation, destruction, power, and protection.

The house is surrounded by complete destructions and devastation.

SLYPH With winds reaching up to 170 miles. It was reported to be the deadliest in the U.S for over five years.

The Slyph Elements of Air.

Slyph are air elements. These are the beautiful clouds in the sky that look angelic.

They form the beautiful features of angels. They look so divine because they are.

One of nature's elementals. Their sole purpose is to clean the air of toxic, harmful chemicals that poison our skies. They are very beautiful with an angelic nature.

I can remember once I was looking at the sky, as I often do. As I am. Watching one of the sylphs, it begins to move downward, and I thought to myself, clouds don't move around in the sky. They just kind of evaporate is disappear. Then it begins to move back upward to the other slyphs in the sky. I was so amazed that I saw it in its glory; it then moved sideways alone in the sky and faded away.

Riddle 1

"I NEVER WAS AND ALWAYS WILL BE.

NO ONE EVER SAW ME, AND NOR EVER WILL.

AND YET I AM THE CONFIDENCE OF ALL WHO
BREATHE AND LOVE:

WHAT AM I??

The answer is at the end of the book.

Sylphs in their natural beauty

Gods in the skies cloud atlas

One day, I decided to take my grandson to the park. As he was playing on the slide, I decided to take more pictures of the beautiful skies. I just love the sky and the clouds; they always look so amazingly beautiful.

If you have read my first book "Amazing Universe, the magical earth we live on. I speak of a day at the park, seeing a bumble bee mourning the loss of his mate this is the same day. I love nature.

I looked up to the clouds. They were beautiful, perfect in colors of blue and white. So, I decided to take some photos of the clouds, as I often do. Later, as I review the photo in one sitting. I have been known to take snap to 30 photos a day as I am reviewing. I see a beautiful goddess baby smiling back at me so beautiful.

My heart was in amazement; this was the first photo I had captured of a spiritual image. I was in a state of awe. She is beautiful.

I thought to myself! Is this real? Am I the only one who can see this image of this beautiful infant child staring at me through the clouds?

Rushed to a friend and showed her the photograph. Her reply was. "yes, that is!

A NEW DAWN

A new dawn was unfolding I didn't understand. My insights were definitely beginning to unfold. I thought," Let's take more photos of the beautiful planet to see where this is leading me too. My quests had begun."

Every place I went, I was photographing the tree, the bushes, the flowers, the birds.

When I spoke of what I was encountering in my photos, people were skeptical; they would say, "You are photoing pictures of shapes, forms that look like people." I would just say," There are gods up there in the skies looking down on us humans.

People's thoughts were. I had lost my mind! If you have ever watched the movie "The Gods. It will tell you there are gods in the sky.

Have you ever witnessed a Hercules movie where Zeus and the other gods are looking down at Earth watching Hercules's adventures, this is so!

I say to the skeptic! Prove your theory; I can prove my mind!

We are here to learn. To love. To ascend.

There is only one consciousness, and it is Christ's consciousness. Know thyself. Go within. Work on your ego. This is the real devil. Not knowing who you are should be the incentive behind change, growth, and expansion in your world.

If you can master and destroy the 13 enemies. You cannot see. Such (the jahid).

1.   Egoism

2.   Arrogance

3.   Conceit

4.   Selfishness

5.   Greed

6.   Lust

7.   Intolerance

8.   Anger

9.   Lying

10.   Cheating

11.   Gossiping

12.   Slander

When you have conquered the 12, you cannot see.

Then you will be able to face the one you can see. Together, they make 13. Since you have defeated the enemies and won your struggle, it is not you who is the enemy.

It is those who still struggle. The greedy, the vein, the arrogant.

Duality:

The intuitive, physiological confusing nature of humankind is two-folded. (Urban Dictionary). It is where envy, jealousy, hatred, and evil thoughts split from spirit. You must bring the body, mind, and soul one in spirit. This is called balance.

We must try to master the ego (duality) always by taking into account positive thoughts. The game ends when we learn to master our ego. There is no more judgment of others. You begin to learn that your reflections on others are your own reflection of self-worth. No negativity will live within because the mind creates reality as a coping mechanism. You begin to attract love because you are love.

Beauty is all around us. I was out at the park today with my son and grandson. I love nature. With the fresh air, I feel at home. As I sat, I watched a bumblebee hoover over another bumblebee on the sidewalk. It was not bothering anyone as they walked by. It was making circles around the other bee.

My son then told me, "Mom, he is grieving." As my eyes followed through downward, his beautiful mate (queen) lay there. It was as though someone had just smacked her out of the sky. There she lay limpness and dying them to share the consciousness. We are all one.

To look at something without opinion is the highest form of LOVE.

We are all Celestial beings living here on mother gaia.

An infant's face

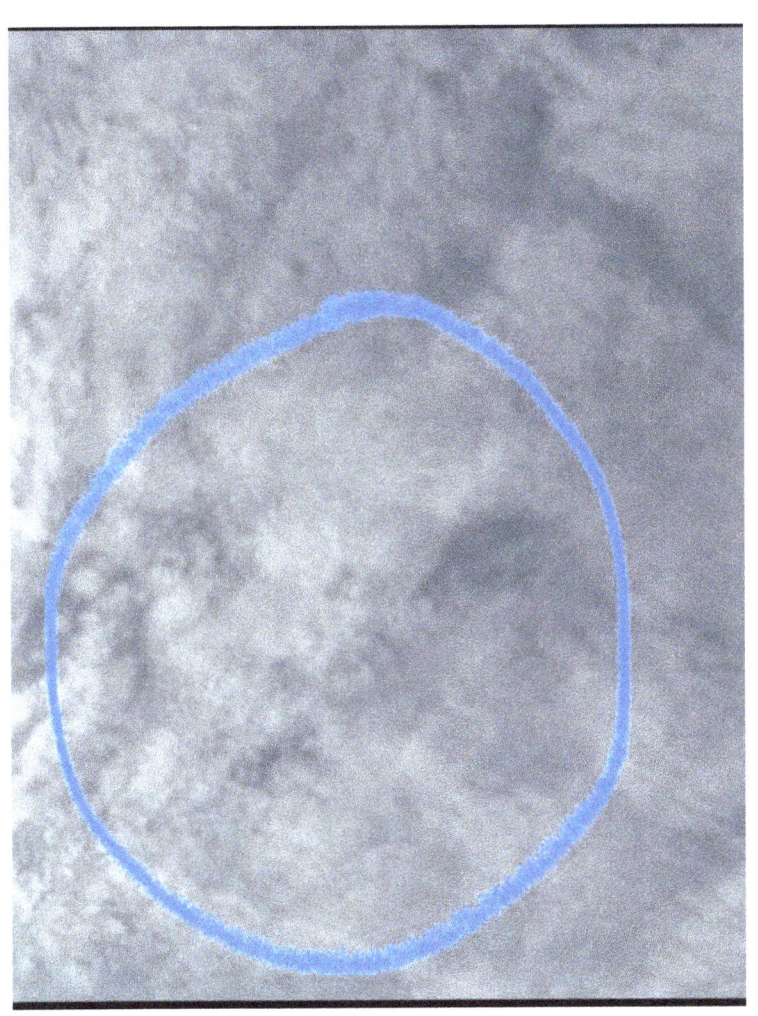

BASTET

The Goddess of the home, and domestic, Fertility, childbirth, and women's secret.

Protects from the home of evil spirits and diseases associated with womanhood. The goddess of pleasure and the bringer of good health. With the head of a Cat and the slender body of a female.

Known also as *The Goddess of the Moon.*

A woman's face

It takes spiritual eye, to see the universe.

An infant's face

Image of an animal in the clouds

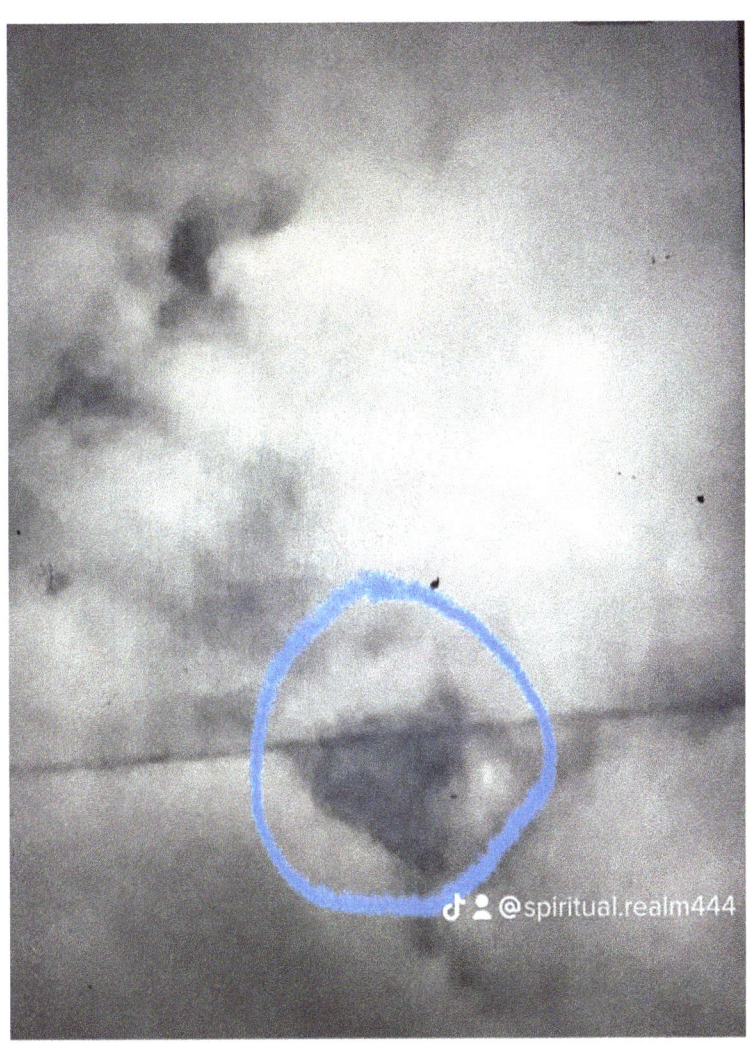

A cat peeking through the clouds.

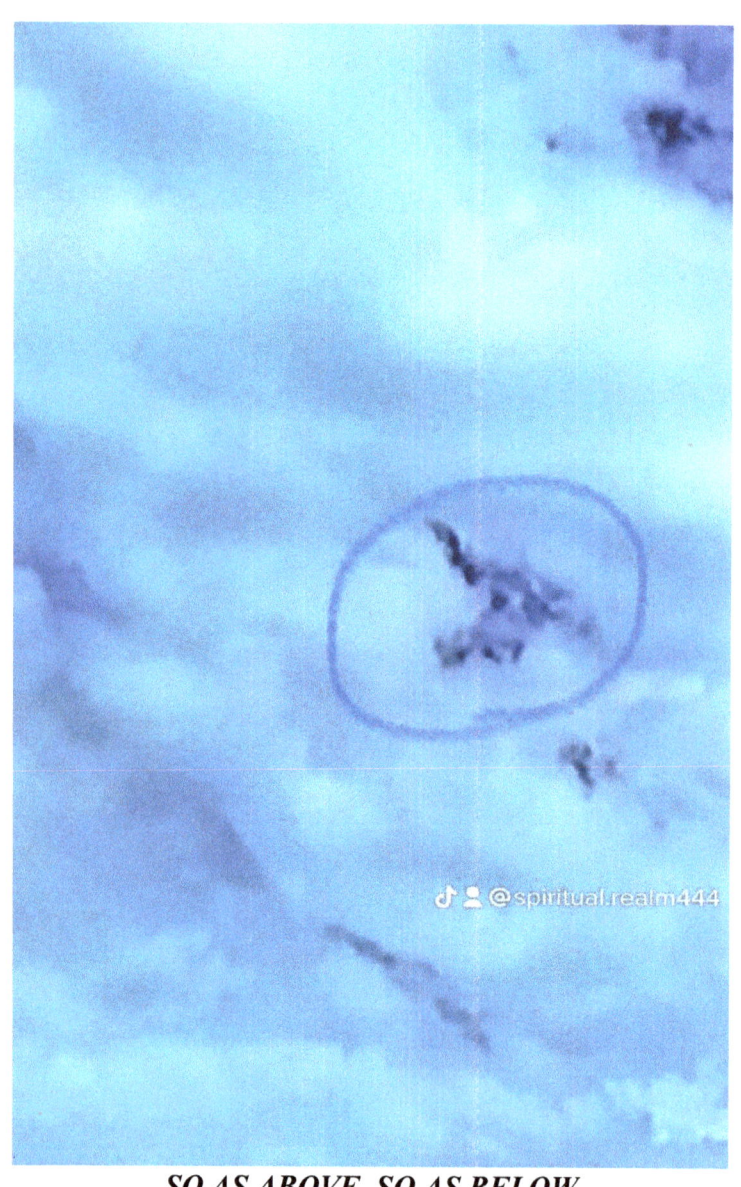

SO AS ABOVE, SO AS BELOW

THE INNATE

The innate. This being is you.

One morning. It was a very beautiful sunny morning as i felt the joy of the day. I was filled with avery good feeling, energized. Dont know where it was coming from didn't bother to question it.

I stood in front of the 40 inches monitor of the surveillance camera. With the images showing in boxes like the one in business used to spy on you in an establishment.

As I was facing the monitor admiring how the day looked so bright and beautiful.

Despite the heartache, I was feeling inside. My oldest sister was in the hospital, fighting for her life. My world. My second mom. She had never visited my home here in Nashville, but she made a promise to me that whe would visit.

As I turned my head away for a quick second and looked by at the monitor, and behold, I saw what looked like a large black cloud moving around in the backyard. I ran, grabbed my phone, and started to snap pictures and videos of the image. The cloud was blinking, changing colors from black to a light shade of grey.

The cloud was glycerine. I shouted out for my partner to come and witness this strange occurrence, but he was always a little fearful.

Look closely into the dark, smokey cloud; you can see an image of a being.

47

There has always been so much energy and activity goin on outside the home; ever since, I built an altar to meditate and pray for all humanity, including Mother Earth.

All the activity was on the south side of the house, where the altar was. We begin to witness big and little orbs rotating around the property. It was so amazing to see.

"IF THE PEOPLE INSIDE YOUR CIRCLE DOES NOT INSPIRE YOU.

INSPIRE YOU.

YOU ARE LIVING IN A CAGE."

SIGILS

Sigils are symbols of power; it is a symbol you use to create or change. That which you charge your energy with intentions to manifest change or desires.

There are some sigils that are pre-made extending back centuries. Invoked with very powerful energies.

For instant, in the occult world, there are certain sigils that are used. They are already associated with certain meanings, spells, inclinations, and certain powers.

These symbols are also used in marketing.

The elite use a lot of the symbols that bring forth good luck, prosperity, and fortune.

There are also sigils that are used for protection. Protection against negativity sent to harm or dismay a person against the evil eye.

The pentagon is also a symbol used in many crafts. A cross is a sigil used just as the cross is used in Christianity for blessing and protection.

Sigils are mostly used in magic.

The term sigils usually refers to a dictatorial signature of a deity or spirit, depending on the outcome you desire.

There are positive, not negative, sigils. Do not pay attention to the things Hollywood deems evil. Such as the pentagon symbolizes protection; it has been used for years by the Wiccan religion and passed down by modern witches through their traditions of ceremony magic. Also worn by pagans as a symbol of faith.

It is believed it started during the mid-evil times. The 5 points are a representation of the wounds of christ.

These symbols come from diverse spiritual paths, including Wiccans, Norse, Judaea, Christianity, Egyptians, and many others.

PROTECTIVE SYMBOLS

Pentacle   Solar cross   Mars sign

Hamsa   Eye of Horus   Triquetra

Bindrune (example)   Hexagram of Solomon   Crossed spears

www.groveandgrotto.com

Crossed Spears

Magical symbols of protection

MAGICAL SYMBOLS OF PROTECTION

HAMSA

This hand-shaped sigil symbol with the eye of Horus is one of the popular madra of the people, especially in the middle eastern of africa. Mostly worn as a necklace. The all-seeing eye of Horus represents healing knowledge and protection from evil.

The palm is said to warn of the evil eye. The open right hand represents power.

THE EYE OF HORUS

The eye of Horus or 'ra is one of the most used protection symbols in history. An ancient Egypt symbolizing power, it is said to protect anything it looks upon. The sun god Amen 'ra represents eternal life and rebirth. This is the reason the church says, "Amen after every prayer. He decreed the people of Egypt to worship him, after every prayer. You are to recite his name (amen), and this mockery is still active in the cogic Christianity religion today.

CROSSED SPEARS

This is simple; there is no mistake in the meaning. The " do not pass" symbol is often used in conflicts and quarrels.

It is used to put up a psychic barrier or block the actions of an adversary.

SOLAR CROSS

It is an equal-armed cross known as the Sun Cross; it is believed to be one of the older Religion symbols.

In the world. With links to Asian Americans and Europeans, It also Has been found on ancient walls amd in places of worship. Coins and artworks as well.

In the Norse culture, it is known as the Odin's Cross, a representation of Odin. The most powerful of the Nordic Gods.

It has been used around the world in many cultures until Hitler appropriated and tainted the one true meaning. For it has serval meaning it sybolizes the Sun, during The Bronz Age it was very active.

Circles

Symbolizes vitality, wholeness, completion and perfection. Circles symbolize the Creation. The Flower of Life. The Alpha and The Omega. The beginning but know the End. The Divine Life force. The nature of the Universe, The birth, and the End.

It explains in depth the cycle of life. In a cyclical universe, happening as a complete set of events that repeat themselves regularly in the same order or in a regularly repeat period of time. This is the Universal way.

Riddle 2

IT CAN BRING TEARS TO YOUR EYE.

BRING THE FORGOTTEN BACK.

"MAKE YOU SMILE & REVERSE TIME.

I FORM IN AN INSTANT BUT LAST A LIFETIME.

WHAT AM I?"

Talisman

A Talisman is usually inscribed in stone. That is believed to have magical powers; these powers are used

for protection to bring good fortune. And to avert The Evil Eye. and bring good luck to the bearer.

There is a mudra, a symbolic hand gesture that is believed to have the power to spread joy, love, happiness, fortune, and protection.

The thumb represents fire, the first fingers represent air, the middle finger represents space, the ring finger represents earth, and you pinky represents water.

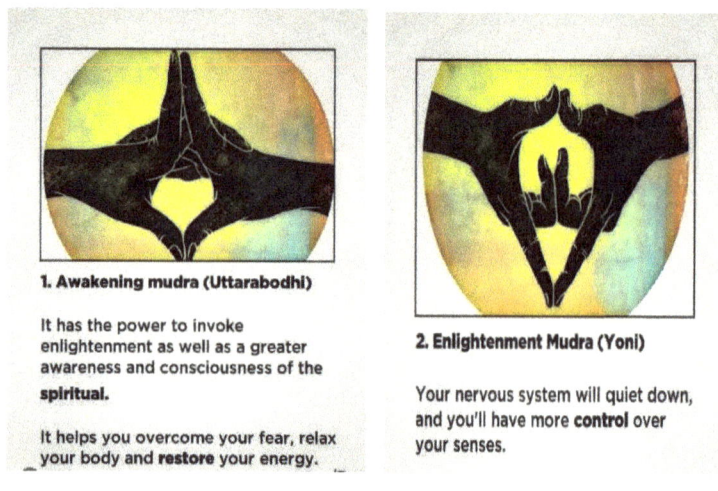

1. Awakening mudra (Uttarabodhi)

It has the power to invoke enlightenment as well as a greater awareness and consciousness of the **spiritual.**

It helps you overcome your fear, relax your body and **restore** your energy.

2. Enlightenment Mudra (Yoni)

Your nervous system will quiet down, and you'll have more **control** over your senses.

3. Illumination mudra (Kalesvara)

It will slow down your thoughts and make you more aware of addictive **behaviors.**

It improves your memory, clears your mind of competing thoughts, and helps you **concentrate.**

3. Illumination mudra (Kalesvara)

It will slow down your thoughts and make you more aware of addictive **behaviors.**

It improves your memory, clears your mind of competing thoughts, and helps you **concentrate.**

5. Kali mudra

It will be useful in getting rid of some unnecessary heart baggage and giving you the strength to get through a **trying day.**

It promotes **optimism** in the body while unclogging channel blockages.

EXPLANATION:

Every organ and bodily part is **connected** to your hands.

Mudras are unique hand motions that, when sustained with **focus,** can directly stimulate healing processes within the **body.**

"We are the offspring of an Ancient Celestial Architects. Why are we left to ponder? Our "Divine

Inheritance."

Ancient teachings share common knowledge. They believe that we all process a divine essence that could be accessed to awakened, for example, the Gnostic text "Pistis Sophia" the wisdom of faith! Speaks of a light that resides in all humans, but it remains in-prisoned in this illusionary world of matter, Gnostics believe it can be assessed and awakened.

We must take a trip down self-discoveries and of the knowing of ourselves of our original potential.

To free our minds of all the Dogma of Religion. An access to the "Divine Wisdom" that lies dormant within our DNA, only through deep meditation and exploration. That we ca begin to unlock the decoding of the mysteries of ourselves and embrace God. (The one Divine Creator). And all the potential that resides within us.

It Is time to access and acknowledge that the Celestial body we inhabitant was designed and created.

By the Anunnaki's (The Pantheon). It is time to stop worshiping them as God the Creator and give them Love and respect. For who they are and for the incredible knowledge they have bestowed on us. (The Emerald Tablets). In doing so, we take control of our own destiny.

We alone are responsible for our own freedom and enlightenment.

"Time waits on; no one ever asks the time.

The time is NOW!"

When it comes to belief and worship, you choose the deity (E Elohim) that best suits your spirituality, heritage, and customs.

Catholics chose The Virgin Mary. Christians choose Jesus. Followers of Islam are called Muslims; they worship the god Allah, Monotheism, which is really Enlil, a Sumerian pantheon. A powerful Anunnaki.

Buddhism worships Buddha.

"Christ will return said Jesus," we are all Christ. The Consciousness of the planet is the inner standing of all wisdom, and ascension is from The One Source. The return of knowledge and wisdom to all human-divine consciousness (the mind). We are One Consciousness meaning that the birds, the Trees, the Insects, the Animal. We are all created the same, we all have Souls. Every living creature on earth has a soul. Why humas think they are so special beats me. This is considered the second coming of Christ. Until your inner stand the metaphor, you are stuck in the Matrix; we are living inside a creation. SOURCE is OMNIUS

12 Laws of Karma

1. The Great Law of Cause and Effect. As you sow. So shall you weep. To receive Happiness, peace, love, and friendship. You must be happy, peaceful, loving and a true friend.
2. The Law of Creation. Life requires our participation to happen; nothing happens by itself. We Are One with the Universe.
3. The Law of Humility. One must accept something in order for it to change the outcome if all you see is negativity. Then the situation will be according to your vibration negative.
4. The law of Growth. Wherever you go, then there you are. It is we who must change, and not the people, places, or things around us. When we change who we are within our hearts, our lives follow suit and change as well.
5. The Law of Responsibility. If there is something wrong in one's life, there is something wrong with them. We mirror what surrounds us, and what surrounds us mirrors us. This is the Universal Truth. You must take responsibility for what is in your life.
6. The Law of Connection. The smallest or the least important things must be done because everything in the Universe is connected. Each step leads to the next step and so forth on and so on.

You must do the initial work to get the job done. Neither step is more important than the other. They are both needed to accomplish the task. The Past, Present, and the Future are all connected.

7. The Law of Focus. One cannot think of two things at the same time if our focus is on Spiritual Values. It is not possible to have thoughts like greed and anger.

8. The Law of Giving and Hospitality. If one believes something to be true. Then, sometime in their lives, they will be called upon to demonstrate that truth. This is the law that makes "you practice what you preach into perspective, about selflessness, helping and giving to others.

9. The Law of Here and Now. You cannot be in the here and now if you are still trying to confront your past. You have to be present. We live in a world full of chaos and distraction. Most of us are more focused on the past than now.

10. The Law of Change. History repeats itself until we learn the lesson; then, we can change our path if we find ourselves in the same situation over and over again. Maybe the law of change is the blame. It is from the universe pushing you toward change.

11. The Law of Patience & Rewards. This law stated that consistent hard work pays off. Achieving great and wonderful things will always require patience.

12. The Law of Significance and Inspiration. The law of significance states that we all have a purpose to offer to the world. Every Soul incarnates with perfected

abilities. Some people are in touch with their divine purpose, while others seem to have difficulty figuring out what their purpose on this earth is. I had an exceedingly difficult time with this law.

WHO CREATED THE 12 LAWS OF KARMA

The roots of Karmic trace back to the Ancient Rigveda days. The oldest known Vedic Sanskrit hymns. Documented around 1500 BCE (before the birth of Jesus).

It is now the principle of Hinduism and Buddhism.

Riddle: 3

'I HAVE A NAME, BUT IT IS NOT MINE.

YOU DO NOT THINK ABOUT ME WHILE IN YOUR PRIME,

PEOPLE CRY WHILE I AM IN THEIR SIGHT,

OTHER LIE WITH ME ALL DAY AND ALL NIGHT,"

WHAT AM I?

HEART OF LOVE

Love is what makes your life worth living.

Love should be all humanities religion. If we would only love our neighbor as we do ourselves.

If we could only see the spirit. The essence of a soul and not the outer appearance, then we would be practicing love. An unbias love for all.

The soul of a being is light celestial. There is not a human being that is black, yellow, white or brown. Some may follow a different path than others. We are all the same. Religion separates us, making one class of people believe that they are better than the other.

Religious wars are heartbreaking. Someone sent me a meme the other day, and it spoke.

"The bible vs the koran. And there is only one creator (source). It is all for control. Be a free thinker. Who needs a book to tell you how to love, live, and respect thy neighbor?

"evil men create disharmony that reaches out and destroys men."

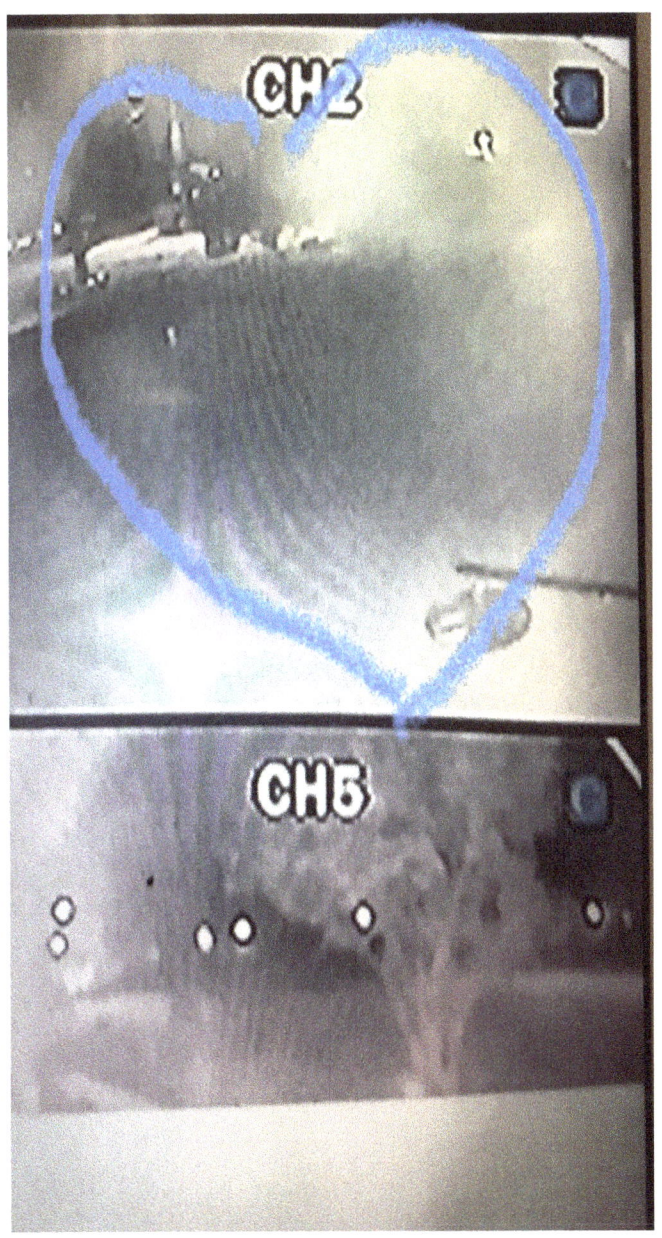

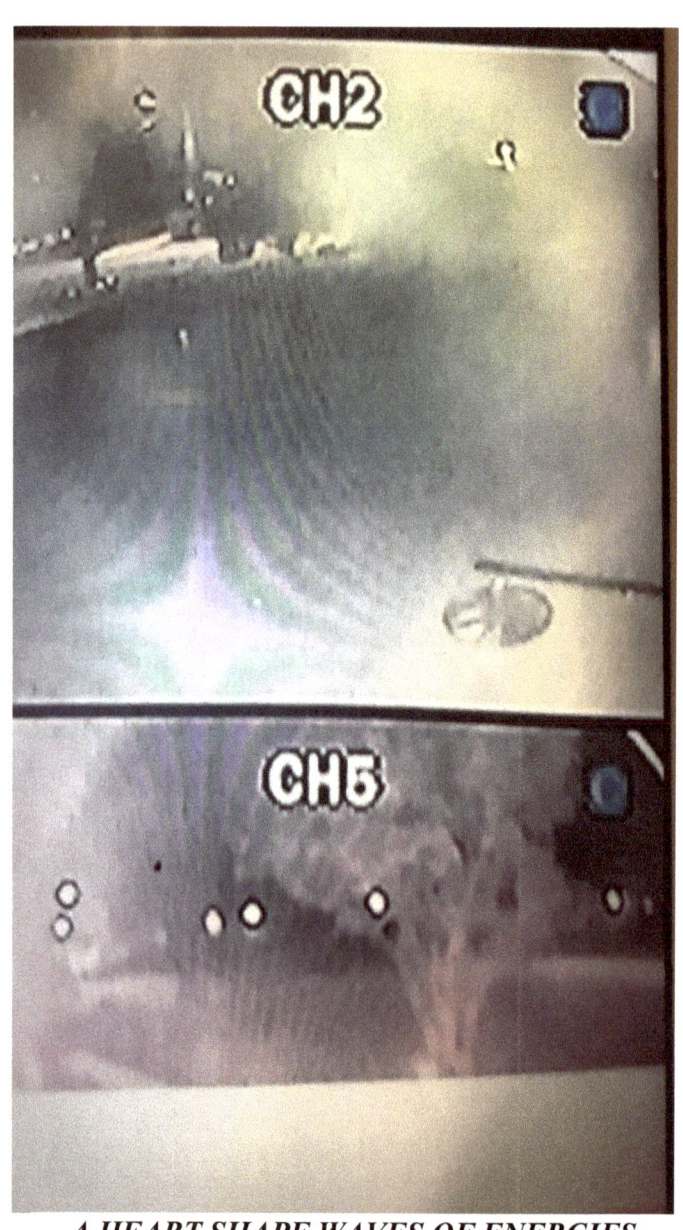

A HEART SHAPE WAVES OF ENERGIES

MAN-MADE RELIGION

PSALMS 147 19-20 (NIV)
19 "he has revealed his word to Jacob, his laws and decree to israel.
20 "They have done this for no other nation; they do not know his laws

Let me introduce you to the creators of religion:

John Smith created the Baptist religion in 1608
Charles Parham created the Pentecostal religion in 1901
Joseph Smith created the Mormons religion in 1830
Charles T. Russles, created the Jehovah's Witness religion in 1872
William Miller created the 7th Day Adventist religion in 1863
Constantine, Christianity's first council of Nicaea 335 AD, was the first Christian emperor. He introduced Christianity to the world. The pagan doctrine of worship.
The Trinity, easter, Sunday worship, Christian cross, Christian fish, lent (40 days after the death of Jesus).
Knowledge is power for freedom. Study to show your self-approval.

WATCHING WAVES OF ENERGY

I was awakened by the most beautiful show of energy. The orbs were dancing, a hundred of them moving in circulation. Waves of energy, all different colors, beautiful colors simultaneously motions very difficult to explain. I have attached a photo for your illustrations.

Very beautiful and relaxing to watch. Every morning, I would awaken, staring at the monitor, waiting for something spectacular phenomenon to happen. This was the beginning of my spiritual journey.

The spiritual thing I have seen. Too chose me to experience such an amazing blessing.

I begin to video, and snap pictures.

But one thing im sure about it gave me such amazing feelings.

Waves of energy waves and frequencies

FAIRIES

Do you believe in fairies, gnomes, mermaid? All the mythical creatures and folktales have some truth and meaning.

These mythical creatures are not a figment of someone's imagination. They live here. Earth, as well. In a different dimension. Or frequency, should I say?

We have all incarnated and have been earth spirits at least one time in our life span, or an animal at one time. Learning and experiencing life. We have experienced every type of incarnation we decide the experience.

A rock, a microphone, a human. It's up to you! We come to Earth School to create, to learn to ascend.

We are master creators, created by the master creator to create here, with creation.

Whatever your gifts are, your passions in this life, these are your creation tools.

Source has given us all a purpose. Source (god of creation) has given us all a purpose; it's up to you to fulfill your destiny of purpose. What's your passion? What do you adore doing without hesitation? What inspires you?

"We are all one in the light of the spirit."

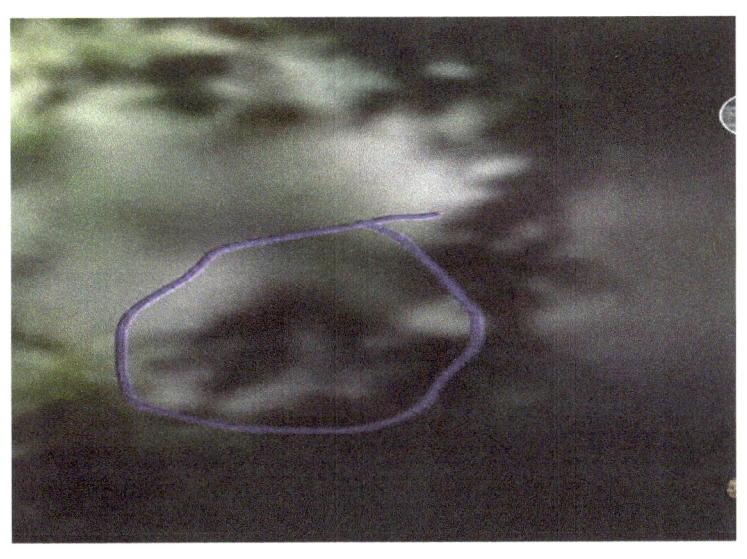

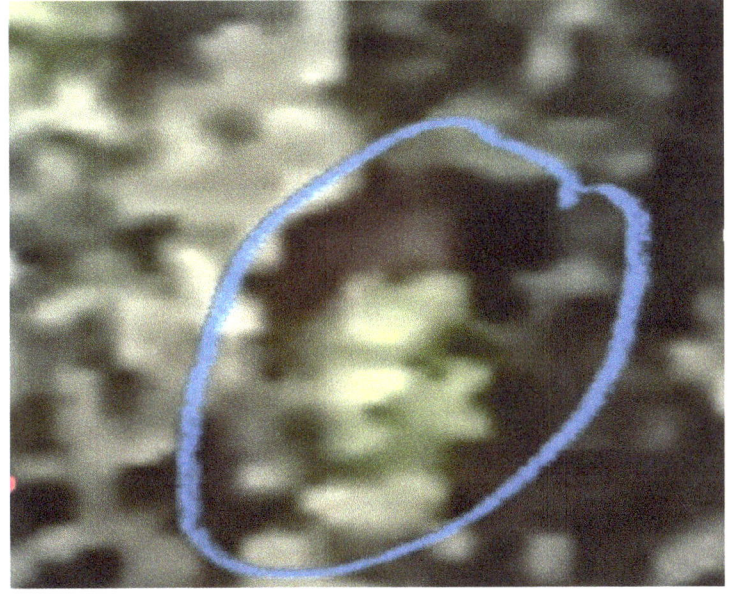

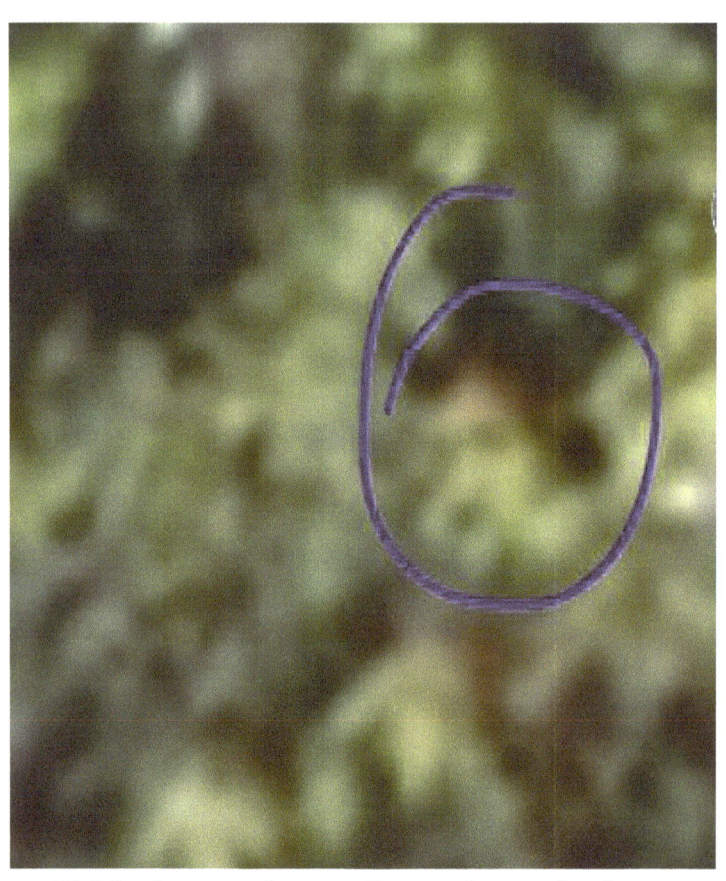

Fairies in a nearby tree. I wear the magic glasses proudly.

"ALL AROUND YOU ARE SPIRITS.
CHILD. THEY LIVE
IN THE EARTH, THE WATER, THE
SKY.
IF YOU LISTEN, THEY WILL GUIDE
YOU"

Pocahontas

WITCHCRAFT

Let's debug what we have been programmed to believe; no one really speaks or questions the real reason witches were trialed and hung, not burned. To worship anything outside the Father, Christianity was punished by death.

You were considered a heathen, pagan devil, and idolatry.

To give thanks to Mother Nature, which is all god. It was considered blasphemy, evil, idolatry, and paganism; the witches knew that elemental and nature were our healing. That all things were god. The word witchcraft originated because it was considered a craft to know the different herbs to mix and leaves and branches and floweres and earth for all healing.

The witches were sought out when plague tormented towns for certain healing ointments and lotions. They created natural medicines. When the plague was in town. Witches were not usually affected by the fever because the main source of the fever was rats dropping and transfering of the deceased. But a lot of females had cats, so if you had a cat, you probably would not have caught the fever because cats chase mice away.

Anything that you are told. Please research and find the truth; a black cat is not a sign of bad luck. But the masses and television have deemed them evil. And black is beautiful. A cat purring its healing; it vibrates a healing vibration.

The witches new that certain natural earth and gems carried energies of the earth. Onyx, jade, sapphire, crystals, emeralds, etc. They were not allowed to possess such beautiful stones without being deemed a witch. It was the knowledge they wanted for themselves.

"That which you take will always.
Be taken from you!

PHOTOS OF THE CLOUD ATLAS

ALL PHOTO WERE PHOTOGRAPH

BY:
RUBY THOMAS

Author of:
AMAZING UNIVERSE
The Magical Earth we live on

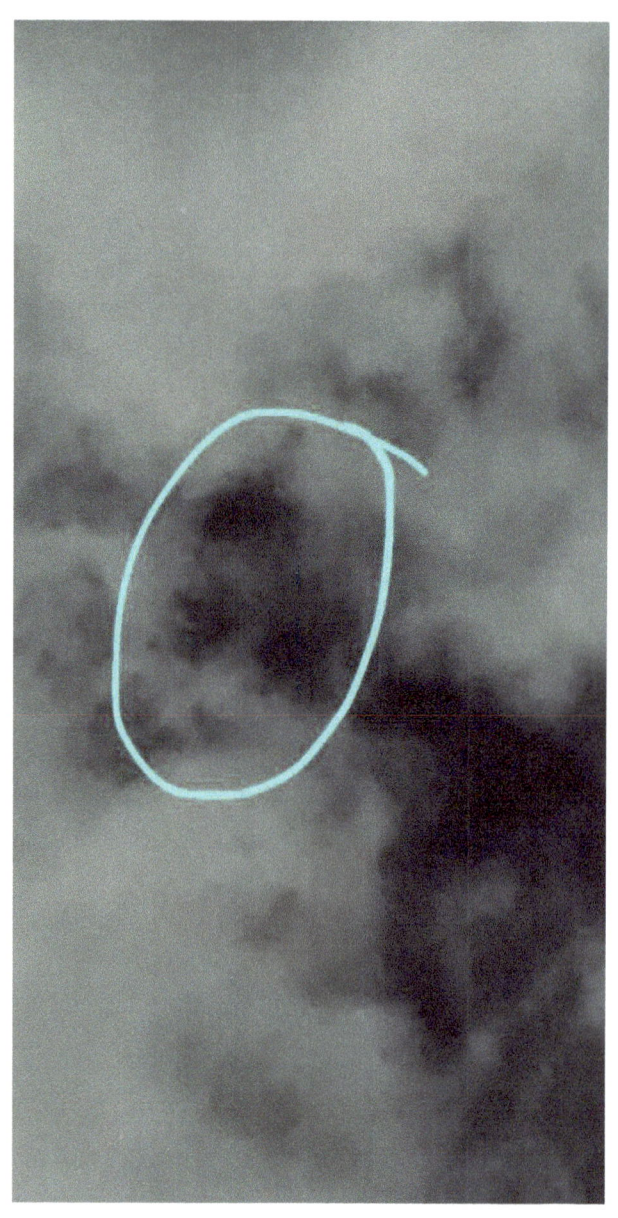

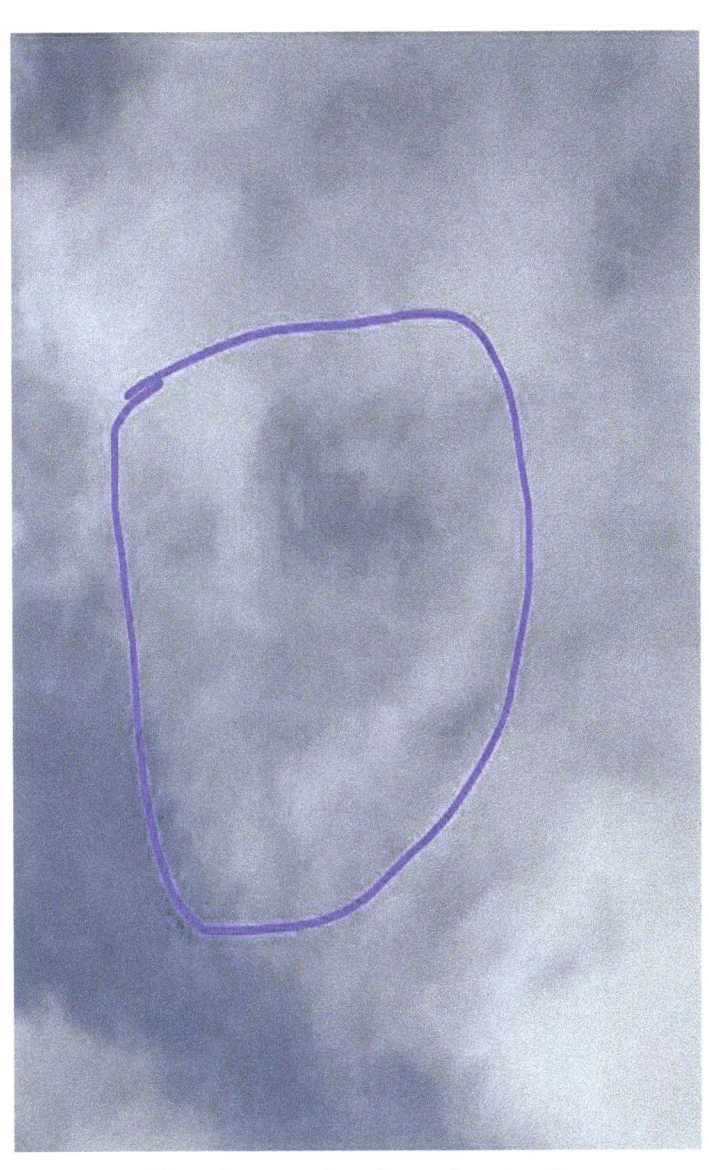

Man, face staring from the clouds.

Can you spot the infant fac to the left of the photo, looks like the Gerber baby?

Eye of Horus

Hamsa

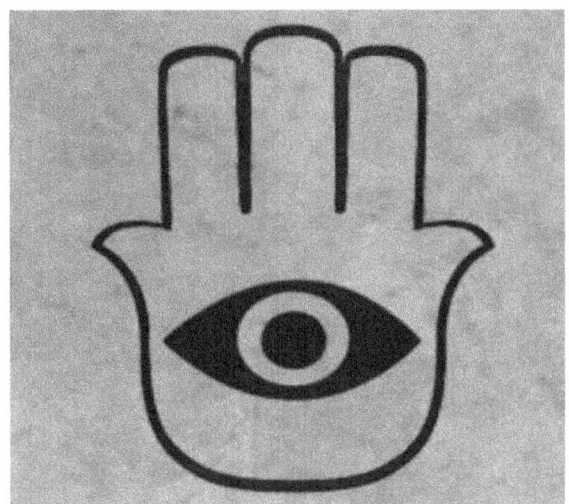

For protection

Can you see the owl?

A Portal

89

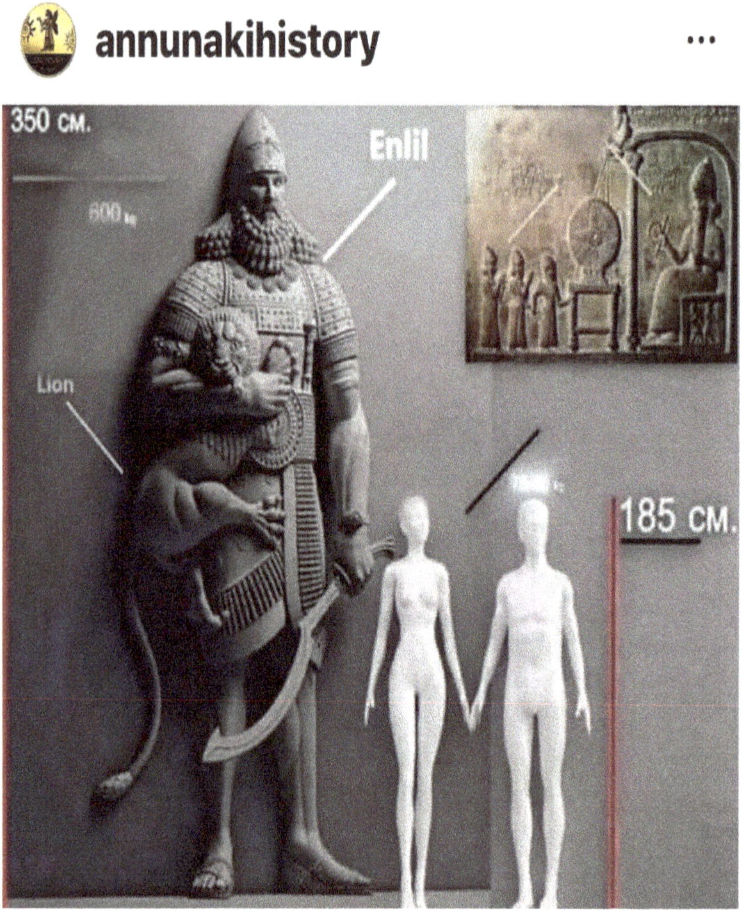

Ancient Sumerian Pantheon, they came from Nibiru (the Red Star)

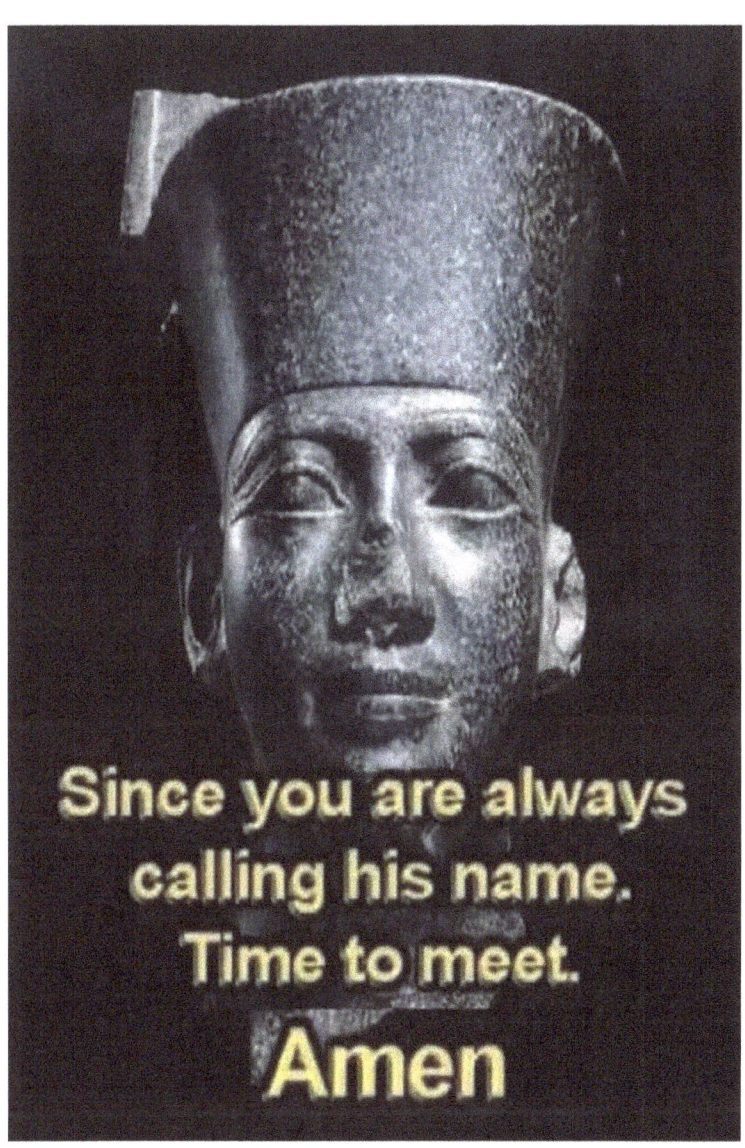

Meet the deity Amen RA/Enlil/lucifer. A Sumerian Parthenon who masqueraded around as good. He decrees that after every prayer, you were to worship and speak his name only. He decreed no more worship of God's monotheism. That he is the one and true God, but he was human. Knowledge from the Ancient Emerald Tablets

ANSWER TO RIDDLE ONE.

TOMORROW.

ANSWER TO RIDDLE 2.

MEMORY

ANSWER TO RIDDLE 3

TOMBSTONE

AUTHOR NOTE

People change at least 5 to 7 times in a lifetime. It is impossible to remain the same.

Until you reach a moment of enlightenment, which usually comes with age and wisdom.

You see, people change us, situations change, family changes us, men in our lives change us.

When we reflect back on the past, then and there, we begin to work on ourselves.

You are awakening to the knowledge that all is within. No one is coming to rescue you from yourself. No god, no Elohim. No savior.

When you change your thoughts, you not only change your mind but your destiny and whatever situations you feel you cannot handle, you are the source at the wheel.

I am the first of my bloodline to break the generational course of religion.

There for I declare my bloodline from this day forward is free. Free from the enslavement of the mind, body, and soul. From the incarnations of knowing who they are.

Protect your energy at all costs. Do not allow a person's perception of you to trigger any unhealed pain.

It is part of the perception you agree with that triggers pain and resentment.

Stop with the emotions and the commotions.

The eye has shades that only the dying is supposed to see. I died one afternoon,

My heart stopped. I was able to see and experience these window shades closing.

In a vertical direction.

I have come to the conclusion, life is about finding your balance. Adding to your character to enhance your life and your soul.

You must not go through life thinking you don't need to change who you are. That god made you like this. This is ignorant thinking.

This is just another way to accept the flaws of being human, making up excuses for your actions, and then putting your actions on to another person, "the devil made me do it! No accountability for your own choices.

No, being human, we are also prone to outside forces! Of negativities. But in the end, the choice is yours.

Finding a balance in life will keep you on a positive path. Not allowing others to dictate who you are.

The majority of people call it soul searching. I call it balance.

You have to find a balance point in your life so that the world you live in won't become part of you! The fears want to become part of you. You can see through the mask of deception.

You will be able to balance the positive and negative parts of this life.

This is the 'pursuit of happiness.'

If you pursue your happiness, it very seldom finds you.

Utilize that god giving a gift you were giving called a brain when you release the problems. The brain will give you more areas of solutions; it is meant to enhance your life, not to take away.

It is our free will, so choose wisely.

Whatever is for you will definitely draw toward you. This is called synchronicity.

But it's not going to beat you over the head to get your attention. This is where being balanced comes into play.

We are the temple of god; why do you suppose that the small area on the sides of your forehead is called a temple and the top of your head is called the crown….

Because we are the temple god….

"Your flesh, This rock, The stars in the sky. All things in the cosmos are made from the same Atoms.

From the moment we are born. We all hold a Cosmo within ourselves."

"Knights of the Zodiac"

THINKING OUT LOUD

In a world full of imperfections, there is perfection.

There is no quick fix or easy road in life.

There are no manipulations in life.

There are no lies in life.

There are no short corners to life.

There is no scheming in life.

There is only you! And you only can change your destiny. You are not what the world thinks of you. You alone are the only one who can make a change.

Choosing to go about life in the wrong direction will cause you to change drastically in life.

This is the reason so many people are suffering today because of their choices.

For every action, there is a reaction, whether it's positive or negative. You will reap the benefits.

Life gives to the givers and takes from the takers…

It is about how you play the game of life. It is not a fact that a god blesses some and not others.

I know that you skeptics are going to have a field day with this one.

It is about how bad you want it. And the extent you are willing to take to get to it.

Bad things happen to good people as well. There is no one to blame. You cannot blame a god for the good things and a devil for the bad things that happen.

I was sitting outdoors in my vehicle. Enjoying the quietness. And my pondering took off.

I said to myself. Why do I live in poverty?

Please do not take this out of context. The universe has been good to me, and I am very thankful for what I have. I live in a beautiful city, a nice 2-bedroom apartment. I own my car, a Cadillac SUV, and I am still poor.

So, my thoughts took me on a journey. I went from a young child and a young adult to now, and all above and beyond.

I then pondered over the talk show hosts Oprah Winfrey, Tyler Perry, Wendy Williams, and so many other celebrities and billionaires and millionaires who once lived a life of poverty and what was so special about them that they had reached a status in their lives where they control their destiny. Their dreams had all become their reality.

I said to myself. We walk the same path of life. Being born into the world. And Once you reach a certain stage you have to walk the walk alone.

What is so different about you? That is not worth me.

What do you do to win the favor of the creator? If we are all created equal.

What did you do or say to the universe that has made you prosperous, affluent and bountiful of goods, a cup running over with all your true heart desires?

Here is my answer:

They use the laws of the universe. "the inspired action." They become inspired to change their lives and their destiny, and they put in 100% work in the action of the universe.

They became creators. Inspired to change the world. And where there is action, you are now speaking the universal language.

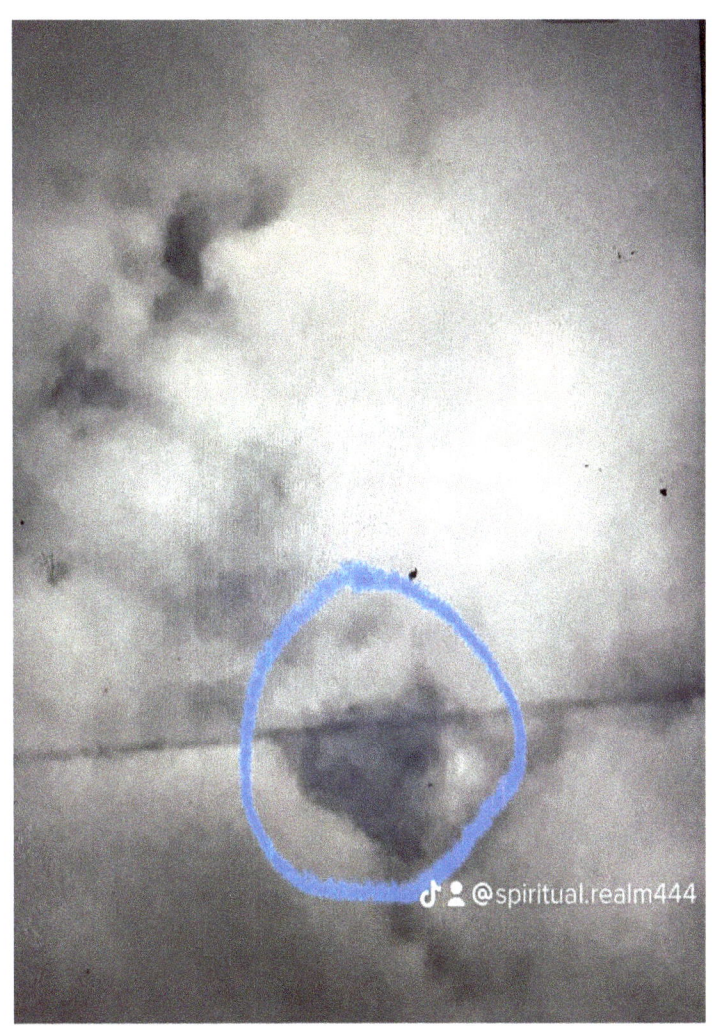

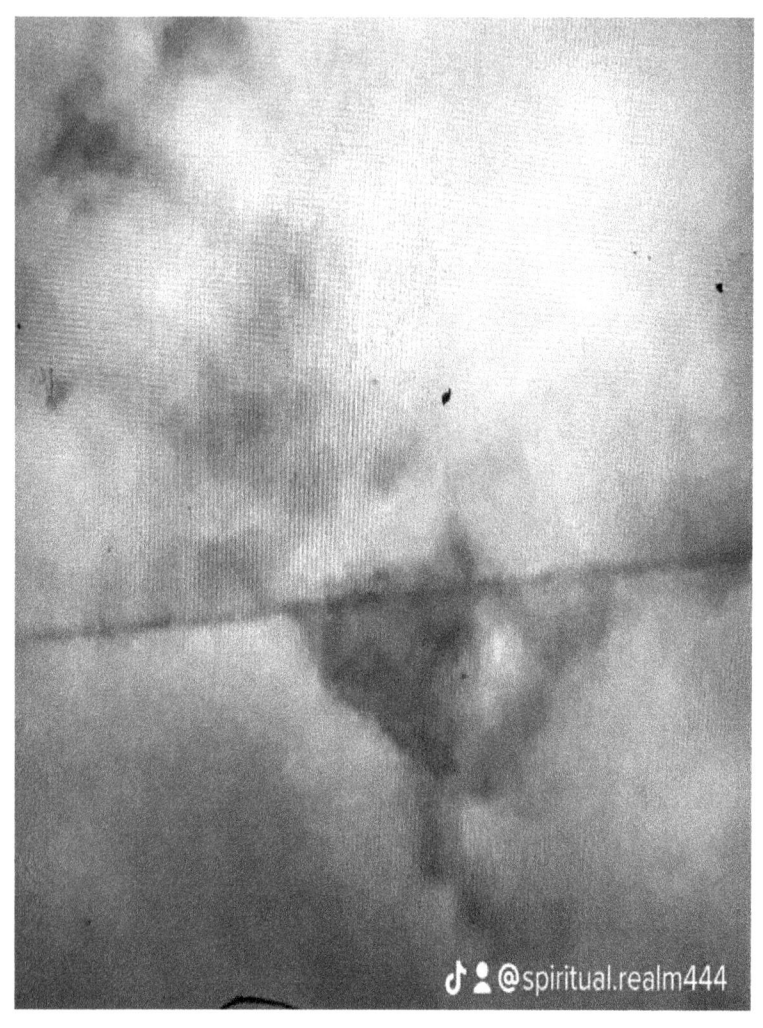

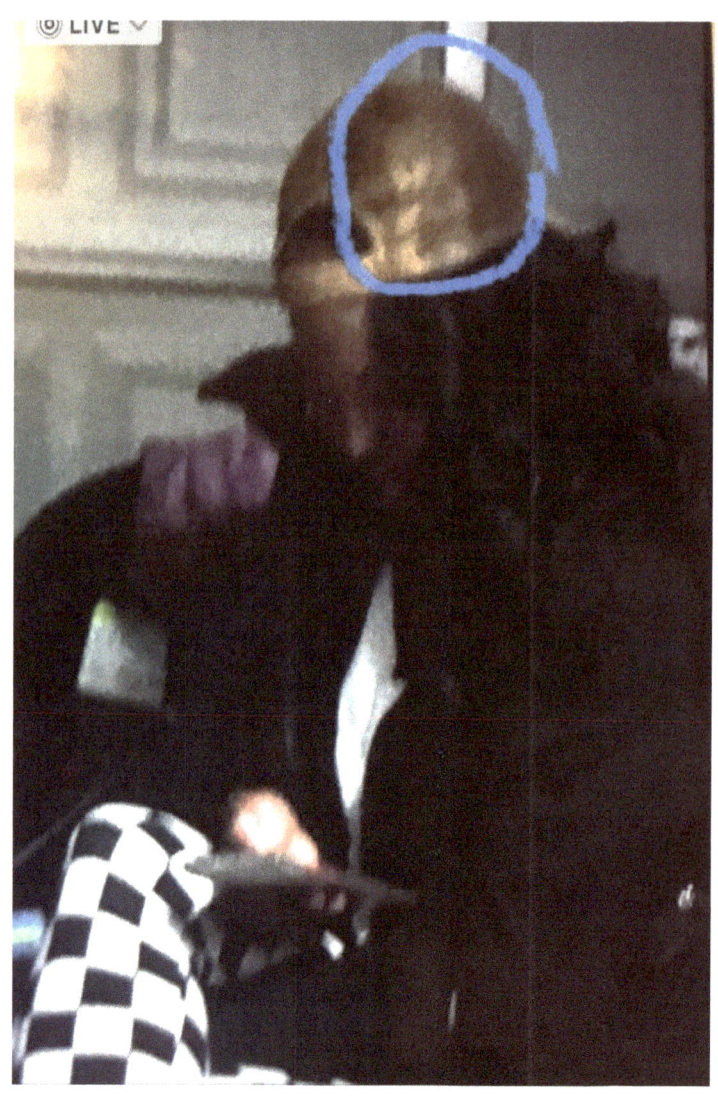

As I begin to dive a little deeper into my spirituality. I decided to make my dining room into an altar. To give thanks and supplications to pray for the healing of Mother Earth (Mother Gaia), her true name.

She is alive.

Once my alter was completed. I begin to pray every day at the same time, remembering to always give thanks for the good and the unfortunate occurrences. To see good in all things.

I would meditate before I begin for approximately 15 minutes before prayer.

Burning incense of myrrh, sage, dragon blood, frankincense, white sage

And praying from within me.

Religion teaches incense is of the devil, related to evil. This, too is a lie, trick of the mass.

FRANKINCENSE has been used since ancient times to help aid in healing the body and soul; it is used for meditation and cultivating inner peace. And also has antigens to help strengthen the lungs. Also related to holiness and righteousness.

MYRRH is an ancient practice. Just like frankincense, they reduce airborne bacteria counts up to 70%.it also stimulate the immune system to make more white blood cells that also kill bacteria,

DRAGONS BLOOD, used for digestive health, is a plant resin formerly said to cure all properties. Once thought to speed up the healing process in wounds. Its use has a variety of health benefits: fever reducer, stops stomach ulcers, and antiviral (medications that help your body fight off certain viruses that can cause disease). It can also be bought in oils.

This plant is grown in South Asia, east Africa, Canary Islands, the West Indies and also South America.

We all know **SAGE** is used for removing negativities; sagings were originally practised by the indigenous people. It is said to purify your space to rid them of negative energies and promote healing and wisdom.

It can also aid in memory loss, diabetes, sore throat, high cholesterol and many other conditions.

WHITE SAGE is a very rich compound that activates certain receptors in the brain; reducing stress and elevation mood levels can also help in reducing pain. It also purifies your space, promoting healing and wisdom.

It's also called smudging.

Once I open my altar to the god of the universe, the creator, the source is what I like to address the creator as, or the one.

That's when I began to notice all the activities around my house. Especially the corner of the house where my alter resides.

At night-time, the universe awakens, and there was a lot of activity after the darkness crept in. I would sit and watch the monitor around our home.

With my phone in my hand, ready to snap the photo, I realized that it was necessary to be ready at all times.

One morning when I was watching the monitor, sipping my coffee. There were 4 spirits flying around in the backyard. Kind of looks like large male sperm. They were all white, coming down into the backyard and returning upward to the sky.

By the time I reached and called for my fiancée to see, they had vanished.

So, I believe it was only meant for me to see.

I began to feel a need to tell the world. I just didn't know how.

You see, I saw all the things that were occurring as a blessing. That my angels and ancestors were around me, protecting me. And they are certainly getting my attention, all these beings of light.

We are all master souls. We chose earth school. To take on a physical form.

In the spiritual realm, it is made up of energy. Orbs are the energy of light. In other words, they are us. Our loved ones, angels, relatives, and ancestors.

We are of light.

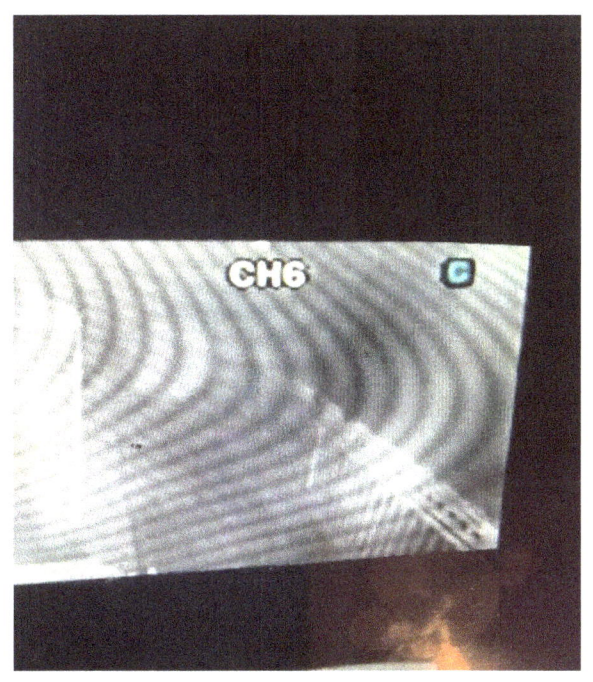

ORBS BEING OF LIGHT

There is individual awareness with every orb. I am sure we have all captured one in a photo. Each one is an objective of the light of consciousness, the soul. The human eye cannot detect.

You are a being of light. And so are your loved ones and ancestors

And also angels are of light.

Through technology, we are able to see another level of frequency that we would not be able to see with the human eye. I often say if we were able to see the unknown spirit world, we would be frightened of the mysterious planet we live on.

If you look deeply into the orbs some seem to have faces. I have a photo, but the quality would not let me upload the picture.

Ultimately, all is one mind. Once you connect and allow them to enter with love and acceptance. They find great joy in letting you know they are around you.

They may start to perform the movement of waves differently in vibration and colors, all in a synchronizing formation; it is so beautiful.

I wish I was able to upload a video to the book. The only way you can see it is to visit my web page:

@spiritual.realm444

I started to interact with the spheres/ orbs surrounding my home.

The movements begin to change along with the directions and colors

As if they know I am enjoying watching them. They were beginning to dance more in sync, changing from colors blue, yellow, orange and white.

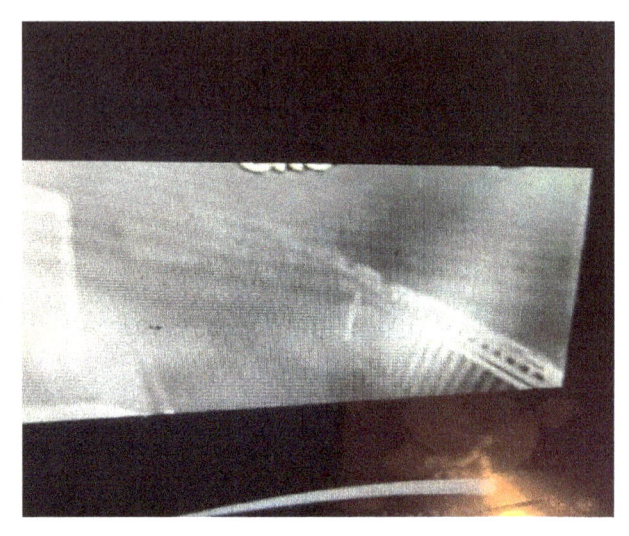

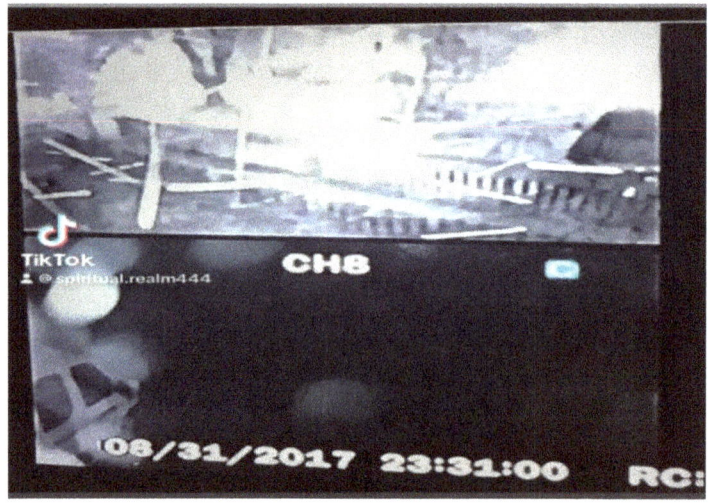

ORBS

"WHEN YOU SPEND TIME WITH PEOPLE THAT

A LITTLE DIFFERENT THEN YOURSELVES.

THERE IS A BIG CHANCE OF YOU LEARNING
SOMETHING NEW!

PRAYERS

I was told as a child that when you pray, your prayers shoot up to heaven like little rockets of light.

I found that to be a fascinating myth. But at that time, I was an adolescent.

I believed in the Santa Clause as well.

I now know the exact meaning of prayers.

Prayers or not, a way of getting unanswered situations or asking for worldly pleasure, such as a husband or a wife. Or to ask for favors.

Or blessing. Money, cars, and house when you pray, you pray to an outside force for help and all is within you to change your situations.

This is why so many prayers go unanswered.

Religion teaches us to pray and ask a god for things in our lives that we have the power to achieve ourselves. Especially to remove your stumbling block.

The creator has given to everyone his/her/ they. A measure of success. It is up to you to search your soul and find your passion.

It could be as simple as being a caregiver. What are you passionate about?

That thing that you can do for hours steals your focus of time. This is your passion.

When you look outside the soul for things that are awaiting or attempting to come to you, you prolong the process.

Prayers are not for salvation purposes. Who on earth needs to be saved, and from what? Evil is a choice. The devil, Satan, this is the ego. We all have free will to choose. Prayers are for gratitude, to show thanks for all there is and what is to come. For the good and the bad, you must see good in all things,

We pray for guides; who do we pray to? Not a sky daddy, for sure.

The god within us all.

We may ask our ancestors for help, guidance, protection, and spiritual blessing; some believe this is voodoo worship. There is no difference to say to a loved one who has gone home to 'watch over your children.

It is the same dialogue. When we pray, it tells the creator that we are thankful. Stop begging and asking for monetary gain, but with a humbleness to life and all there is. Be thankful for all that you have, and what you don't have will definitely make its way to you. Be love, you will attract love, be a blessing, you will attract blessing. It is the law of the universe.

"Devote yourselves to prayers, being watchful and thankful."

Colossian 4:2

Because all is with you.

'They say' religion is not based on fear"! But what happens if you fail to follow the rules?? You burn in a hell.